Memories

Memories

My Parents the Mystics

Sita Earlyne Chaney, Ph.D.

Astara's Library of Mystical Classics

Published by

Astara

792 West Arrow Highway
Upland, CA 91785

Astara, Inc.
792 W. Arrow Hwy.
P.O. Box 5003
Upland, CA 91785-5003
www.astara.org

ISBN 0-918936-47-0
Library of Congress Control Number: 2003103389

Printed in the United States of America
Cover design by Elizabeth Hickerson

Table of Contents

In the Beginning	1
A Most Unlikely Birth	3
Daughter of the Moon, Nokomis	5
Margit and the Sirens	7
Yes, Dear Reader, There Is a Santa Claus	9
There Is No Hell	11
Colorful	13
Sita, Do I Owe You Any Money?	15
Bed of Roses	17
Sisters	21
Sweet Children of the Infinite	23
Heavenly Holidays	25
ET	27
Nature	29
Sing a Song	31
This World and Another	35
Mine Eyes Have Seen the Glory	37
Unhappy Camper	39
Common Folk	43
Here We Go	45
Sacred Sites	47
What's in a Name	49
Shooting Stars	51

Sometimes You Have to Work at It	53
Know Where You Are	57
Stranglers in the Night	61
Kippersita	63
My Medium Dad	65
Born Laughing	67
Mom at the Way Station	69
Stay on 95	71
Rituals	73
Mom Now	75
My Dad's Sermons	77
Right Car, Right Relationships	81
Lights in the Forest	83
A Pat on the Head	85
Big, Bad Me and Mickey D	87
Broken Window Reflections	89
I've Been Truly Blessed	91

Dedication

This book is dedicated to my wonderful mother and father who inspired me to write it by the way they raised me. And to my wonderful big sister, Astara.

It's also dedicated to several people that I love with every fiber of my being and who have loved and supported and helped me in many different ways for years of my life. To sweet and wonderful Nina Aronoff, Ph.D., to Steve Doolittle, to my friends Susan Regas and her husband, Bo Riewerts and their three angelic children, Nicholas, Jennifer, and my fabulous goddaughter, Alexandra, and to my nanny, Margit Nilsson.

Acknowledgments

I'd like to thank the following people, whose behind-the-scenes efforts helped bring my memories of life with two mystics into stories I readily, and gratefully, share with you:

Steve Doolittle
Elizabeth Hickerson
Dean Zakich
Susan Chelgren
Pam Rau

1

In the Beginning

This book is about what it was like to be raised by two wonderful mystics who were new age believers before I was born. Most people come into the new age spirituality by being brought up in a traditional religion and then becoming interested in things like meditation, karma, reincarnation, mind/body/spirit connections and things like that. But my training started even before I was born. When I was still in my sweet mother's womb, my sweet father read to her and to me aloud. He read, so I could hear, *The Ramayana*, which is a Hindu scripture. The heroine of the book was named Sita, who represented the goddess of all womanly virtues. I'm sure I have not lived up to the name, but my parents have certainly raised me from the beginning to be in a family of spiritual seekers.

As Rosalind Russell says in the movie *Auntie Mame*, "Life is a banquet and most poor suckers are starving to death." This book is all about stories of how my parents raised me to know that life is a spiritual banquet. There are spiritual places we can go and pick up energies. They trained me in meditation and prayer. I was raised to believe in not only life after death, but reincarnation, and the healing powers of prayer and of Mother Nature. And how all of life is connected on this planet, as well as the probability of our connection to life on other planets, too.

So, dear reader, know that life is a spiritual banquet and don't spiritually starve to death. Join me in all the stories of how my parents taught me, starting even before I was born — when new age thinking wasn't even popular yet — to not only believe in, but to know within my body the spiritual correctness of the new age movement. Come along, dear reader, and I'll tell you every story I remember of how blessed I was to be raised by two wonderful mystics.

2

A Most Unlikely Birth

The way I came into this world, was rather amazing in itself, given the time that it happened. I was born in 1956 at a time when most or all babies were born in the hospital with a doctor's help, with the father pacing away out in the lobby until after the child was born. My sweet mother refused to have it be that way. She talked my father into being determined to have me at home. They would go to doctor after doctor to ask if he would come to the house to deliver me. And doctor after doctor refused, saying they were both crazy.

Finally, they found a doctor who did agree to come to the house. But thankfully, my sweet father took Red Cross classes in how to help deliver a baby. My poor mother went through 24 hours of labor. I guess I was a bit late getting here, and even though the doctor was there, he was asleep in another room and all my mother and father's yelling could not wake him up. So, it was my wonderful father, and my wonderful mother who delivered me on their own. The doctor strolled in for the last five minutes, after he'd awakened, but even then he was not of much help.

As I mentioned previously, before I was born my father read the *Ramayana* to my mother and myself while I was in the womb. Both my parents were startled to find that when I emerged I looked Asian, with eyes that slanted and rather darker skin than they expected. Of course there's nothing wrong with looking or being Asian, but it was totally unexpected, since neither of my parents are Asian. Dad figured that perhaps they had read the *Ramayana* too many times. But I figure that probably in my last incarnation I was Asian or American Indian, or something like that. After a few days I no longer looked Asian but had all the facial features of both my mother and father.

So, even at the time of my birth, I was welcomed into this world by both my parents at our home. And, as you will read in this book, they have given me a wonderful, spiritual welcome home ever since.

3

Daughter of the Moon, Nokomis

When I was growing up, my daddy used to occasionally quote from his favorite poem, *Hiawatha*, by Longfellow. He did it so often that I can still remember the first few lines of it today. Daddy did this because of the mystical aspect of the poem, and as I can remember it goes:

> "By the shores of Gitchee Gumee,
> By the shining deep sea waters,
> Stood the wigwam of Nokomis,
> Daughter of the moon, Nokomis..."

I was so entranced by these lines that I would keep repeating them to myself. This brought up for me a great interest in Native American Indian spirituality, and in mysticism in general.

I have found that through the years, every once in awhile, I would just be tempted to repeat these words to myself and either say them out loud or privately, in my own head. This seemed to help soothe me or guide me forward on my spiritual journey. So, dear reader, let us know that we are all children of the moon, and stars and sun, as well. Children of the Divine Light.

Perhaps come up with something of your own from a poem or a story or a movie that you can repeat to soothe you, inspire you, and take you further down the path of your spiritual journey. You can use *Hiawatha* if you want, but do know that you are a child of the moon, the Divine Light, and just wrap yourself in this Divine Light every day of your life.

That's what I learned from Daddy often repeating these words out loud to me and Mama. Think about saying whatever words fit you to loved ones around you to help share with them the Divine Light within you.

4

Margit and the Sirens

When I was about three years old, my parents were fortunate enough to be able to hire a nanny for me. Both Mama and Daddy paid me plenty of attention and took time out of their work schedule to spend time with me. But Dad was busy getting books published, writing, speaking at seminars, giving sermons on Sundays, and running Astara with my mom. She was busy writing Astara's Degree Lessons, writing her own books and running Astara with Dad. Our whole family was blessed when Mom and Dad were able to hire a nanny from Sweden named Margit. She has been a dear family friend ever since. The time I spent with my parents was wonderful, as was the time I spent with Margit.

When I was young, one of the things I used to do was run screaming in fear to Margit or Mom or Dad whenever I heard a siren. I would even wake up in the night and run to one of them.

Margit and I were out one day when I was about four, and she noticed a police car parked by the side of the road. The police officer sat in the car, probably on his lunch break. Margit was and still is a very kind, loving and wise woman. She was holding me in her arms, and she took me over to the police car.

She said, "Officer, this is Sita, and she gets very frightened when she hears sirens going by. Can you explain to her please, officer, why the police use sirens?"

He answered by saying, "Hi, Sita. I use my siren when I'm going to help people."

Margit said, "Thank you, officer, and what is your name?"

He answered, "Jimmy."

A few days later Mom, Dad, Margit and I were sitting in the living room and some sirens roared past the house. I didn't move from the couch, or cry or yell out in fear.

Dad looked at me and said, "Sita, are you okay?"

And I said, "Yes, Daddy, it's only Jimmy going to help someone."

So, dear reader, when you are startled in your life by something, when you are afraid, when something unnerves you, talk to people about it or meditate on it and try to re-frame it in your head some way. If it's appropriate, know that it's God's way of sending Jimmy to help someone.

5

Yes, Dear Reader, There Is a Santa Claus

When I was growing up with my parents, they were, of course, very spiritual people. But they had wonderful senses of humor, too, and I learned to have one also.

At Christmas time when the poem said, "The stockings were hung by the chimney with care," we not only had little Christmas stockings to hang out, one for each of us, but I would hang up a pair of panty hose by the fireplace also, just for fun.

When I was much younger, my parents started this tradition of not only giving some Christmas presents from Mom and Dad, but an occasional gift would have a tag on it which said, "To Sita, from Sandy Claws." We all laughed about this every year.

In our house, however, we all did believe there was a real Santa Claus. My parents explained to me when I was very young that he wasn't an elf up in the North Pole, but he was the Divine Spirit of Giving. This spirit would whisper in their ears what I wanted for Christmas so they would go out and get it for me. So I never was one of those kids that believed in Santa Claus when I was very young only to be told as I grew older that he didn't really exist.

"Yes, reader, there is a Santa Claus," and he flies divinely on his sleigh into each of our heads and hearts to tell us what to give our loved ones.

So any time during the year, no matter what religion you are, you can tune into this dear Divine Spirit of Giving and give to yourself and the loved ones around you. You may even wish to label the gift, "From Sandy Claws."

6

There Is No Hell

When I was very young I went for a drive in the car with my parents. They were sitting up front and I was sitting in the back seat. I looked out the window enjoying the view and sort of listening to their talking together about religious philosophy.

Mom brought up to Dad how extremely conservative Christians still believed in some souls going to hell, and in the reality of sin. She, of course, did not believe in that.

All of a sudden, I spoke up and said, "Mommy and Daddy, you know there's no such thing as sin." My parents had not taught me that when I was that age.

Dad pulled the car over and stopped, and they both turned around and looked at me amazed. They said, "How do you know?"

And I said, "God told me. People make mistakes, but there's no such thing as sin that would send anyone to hell. There's no hell."

Both my parents looked with amazement at me and at each other.

What I believe now is that when we are born, and when we're still young, we have memories of things we were taught when we were in heaven. As I've grown older, of course, I've learned from my parents about reincarnation and karma, and debts we owe and many, many things like that. I think what I said that day when I was so little was one of the Divine lessons I had learned when my soul was on the higher plane before reincarnating.

Although I have learned almost everything spiritual from my parents, at least when I first got here I was to able to contribute a bit to the conversation.

7

Colorful

When I was a little girl, I heard my mama refer to her parents as "Mama" and "Daddy." She was raised in the South, and as they say, "You can take the woman out of Texas, but you'll never take Texas out of the woman." Just as she did, I still most often refer to my parents as Mama and Daddy. Not because I'm infantilizing myself, but because one of my dear parents grew up referring to her parents that way. So, often in this book that's the way I refer to them.

When I was about eight, my daddy went off on one of his many speaking engagements. It was somewhere across the country, and as they say, "It was a dark and stormy night" when he was flying home. Mama and I got so worried because he was very late coming home from the airport and it was pouring down rain. He finally arrived home safe and sound. And as he always did when returning from a trip, he gave me a gift. The gift was a beautiful doll with a lovely jacket on. The jacket had every color under the rainbow in it. So I named the doll Colorful. My wonderful parents used this doll to impress upon me one of the most important lessons in life. They used Colorful's jacket to tell me that there is a lot of diversity on our planet. There are people of many different races, two genders, many religions, different sexual orientations, and some people who make more money than others. I was taught to value all these differences and to respect them.

Just as Martin Luther King, Jr.'s message to us was, "Let's judge people by their character, not by the color of their skin," let's judge everything by character, but know there's good and not-so-good in every category. Let's all welcome and respect and value the wonderful diversity we find on this little planet of ours. I find people of a different background than mine interesting. So if you do that, dear reader, the world will be just as my doll, wonderful and colorful.

8

Sita, Do I Owe You Any Money?

When my dear mother was ill — in the days her soul was soon to pass from this life — I would sit by her bed as long as twenty hours day, just holding her hand. Most of the time she slept, but occasionally she would wake and have lucid moments. She'd squeeze my hand and say, "I love you, Sita." And, of course, I'd tell her how much I loved her in return.

On the day she passed on, she woke up and squeezed my hand, and with her eyes very clear, she looked into mine and said, "Sita, do I owe you any money?"

At the time, I didn't understand it, because Mama never borrowed any money from me a day in her life.

I said, "No, Mama, you don't owe me any money."

Then she looked at Daddy, who often sat next to me during this vigil, and she asked him "Robert, do I owe anybody any money?"

He said, "No, Earlyne, of course not." And she smiled and fell asleep again.

That was really her last lucid conversation. About four o'clock the next morning, I suddenly woke from sleep. I had awakened every other morning for weeks feeling so sad because of what had been happening to Mom. But somehow, that morning, I awoke feeling happy, I couldn't tell why. I felt her presence in the room with me, and thought, "Well, I'd better check on Mom before I go back to sleep for a few hours." When I checked on her, the night nurse that we had hired to stay with her from midnight on said that twenty minutes ago Mama had asked for a Kleenex, but as I looked at her, it was really clear that her spirit had left her body and she wasn't breathing. Mama had gone to the Higher dimensions of life.

Of course, I was deeply sad at losing her, and I thought back to what she had asked me. I realized she wasn't talking about money, but did she owe me or anyone else any karmic debt. She had been speaking metaphorically, and we had reassured her she was all clear. And so, she was ready to go into the Light and make her way to the Higher Planes.

I understood that feeling of happiness I had woken up with was Mama's spirit trying to reach me and tell me that she had just passed. And in fact, later that day I found a note that she had written several weeks earlier which said, "The moment I make my passing, I want to reach you and let you know. I'll try," it said. Well, she succeeded.

And my answer to her spirit is still, "No, sweet Mama, you don't owe me any money. I owe you for so much love and thankfulness for the sweet way you raised me."

9

Bed of Roses

I don't want to lead you to believe, dear reader, that growing up with two parents who did the kind of work they did was all wonderful and delightful. Most of it was a blessing, of course, not only in what they were doing, but the wonderful way they raised me. But it wasn't all like that.

I was born in 1956, long before Mama and Daddy's type of work was generally accepted. I remember when I was little going to grammar school and the other kids and I would talk about our parents and what they did. When I told them what my folks were doing, they all laughed and made fun or treated me terribly. The children of fundamentalist Christian families among them said my parents were evil, and that we would go to hell, and that I should be ashamed of what they were doing. I learned from a few of these experiences never to talk about what my parents did, with anyone. In fact, in a way, I longed to say something like, "Oh my parents sell insurance."

It was also hard because so many people had their own expectations of me. Most Astarians, of course, treated me wonderfully, and still do. But I remember when I was about ten years old. It was Sunday and I had just finished attending one of Dad's sermons at church. A woman saw me in the little lobby of Astara's temple in Los Angeles after church and started yelling at me. She said, "When are you going to start speaking like your father? And writing like your mother? Why aren't you doing your job?" And I just stood there amazed and feeling somehow guilty that I wasn't living up to her expectation of what I was supposed to be doing, even at that age. Mom and Dad, of course, sweetly said that was ridiculous and for me not to worry about it. But in a way, when I was young, I felt like I was supposed to live up to thousands of people's expectations, rather than simply being who I was. My parents counteracted these feelings when I would speak to them about it and as I grew up, I began to feel much more comfortable.

Still, though, I would not tell my friends at school what my parents did or what Astara was. This finally changed one day, in graduate school, when some dear friends were vacationing up in San Francisco. They were all visiting with the brother-in-law of one of these friends. I was in California, too, visiting my parents. I called up there at the brother-in-law's house to make arrangements for us all to get together. Someone answered the phone and called out to the others, "It's Sita!" The brother-in-law looked up startled and said to my friend, "You mean 'Sita Chaney,' Robert and Earlyne's daughter of Astara?" He ran a metaphysical book store in San Francisco and not only knew of but really appreciated my parents' work.

All my friends were shocked and amazed because *they* didn't know what my parents did. But they responded to me with great interest and support and fascination at what Astara was and my parents' roles as founders. They all came over for a tour of Astara and to meet my parents and were very sweet to me about it. From then on, I learned that it was more than okay to stop pretending that my parents were insurance sales people, but to tell my friends what they did and to actually be proud of it. By this time, of course, metaphysical ideas had gained more general acceptance and most everyone I told was really interested and very respectful of Astara and what my parents did.

So growing up with Astara as my big sister (because they had founded it five years before I was born) wasn't all a bed of roses, but has become one. A wonderful garden enriching my soul, and my parents standing by me the whole way.

10
Sisters

As I mentioned in a previous story, dear reader, when I was very young, Astara seemed like a big sister to me. I experienced all the pluses and minuses having a big sister can bring. My parents did found Astara five years before I was born.

So, when I was growing up, I'd often want to go away on vacation, but Mama said she couldn't until she finished writing the Third Degree. Or Daddy would be away for a long time because he was giving seminars across the country and I missed him very much. So at times I was a bit jealous of my big sister, Astara, and all the attention she got from my dear, wonderful parents. Of course I got wonderful attention, too, which I did appreciate.

It wasn't until I was about twelve that I started working at Astara during the summer months. I stuffed envelopes, and I worked in the book store in Los Angeles, where Astara was located for the first twenty or so years. And I met wonderful members there in the book store who told me how helpful

Astara's teachings had been in their lives. I got to read letters that came in from Astarians that talked about wonderful healings that had taken place, and how much people valued my parents and Astara. It became clear to me in a way that had not been clear before. I was no longer jealous of my older sister, but felt blessed to be in her presence along with my wonderful parents.

I still feel blessed to this day and have jokingly said to my parents that it wasn't that I chose them for parents before I was born, as we do believe happens, but that a bunch of little souls got together, clamoring to be my parents' child, and I got lucky and won the lottery. I remain so proud of my parents and all the work that they've done and what Astara has done for so many people around the world that I feel blessed to be their child and to be associated with Astara. I'm proud of my parents and my older sister and proud of you, too, dear reader, for you are a seeker on the spiritual path, and I think that means we've *all* won the lottery.

11

Sweet Children of the Infinite

When I was growing up and I would give my father a gift for Christmas or his birthday or do some other kind of favor for him, he would always respond by saying, "Thank you, my dear, sweet child of the Infinite." Ever since I've grown up he's occasionally said this to other people on our staff or volunteers at seminars and so on, but when I was growing up that saying somehow helped me stay on the spiritual path, respect myself and feel very connected with the Divine Being.

So remember, sweet reader, Daddy's words, for we are all sweet children of the Infinite, connected with the Divine Being and connected with each other. You are my brother or sister, and we are all on the spiritual path together. Let's keep walking up that path as sweet children of the Infinite together.

12
Heavenly Holidays

I was blessed with parents who made holidays heavenly.

About a week before Christmas my mom would set up a huge table on the patio and beautifully wrap all the Christmas gifts. Somehow she learned to make these extravagant bows, and they were gorgeous. So a famous saying at my house at Christmas, when we were opening the gifts one by one was, "Don't forget to save the bows." Then we'd throw a bow into a box so it could be touched up and used again the following year.

My favorite thing about the holidays, though, was these delightful hunts that my parents would send me on. Every Christmas morning, when I woke up, I would get out of bed to find little candy bars on the floor, one after the other, leading in a zigzag pattern from my bedroom down the stairs to the living room where, of course, Santa Claus had put all the gifts under the tree overnight. So it was wonderful to follow this path down to where all my wonderful Christmas gifts were.

At Easter I'd have an Easter egg hunt in the back yard of our house. I would run with excitement and joy to different parts of the back yard, always looking and always finding wonderful colored eggs and candies, and little Easter gifts. There would always be a teddy bear or another doll sitting in one of the trees in the back yard, and they were wonderful to find, too.

So they made both those holidays again, sort of a metaphor for being on the spiritual path. As we walk together down the spiritual path, dear reader, remember to save any sweet bows, meaning sweet moments in your life, to experience again — a memory of a location, if it's a special, wonderful place, or with a special, wonderful person. And don't forget the spiritual path also is like an Easter egg hunt — we find something colorful and wonderful at every turn and always with a sweet teddy bear as our guardian angel or a Divine Master Teacher watching over us from the trees above. Let the path be just a joy, as it should be, for all of us.

13
ET

A few days ago I rented the movie ET to watch on my video player at home. I was twenty-six when I first saw the movie with Mom and Dad. We all three loved it. Even though I was twenty-six, my parents bought me a sweet ET doll, which I love to this day.

Seeing the movie again the other day reminded me of when I was very young. My mother came to school on some sort of day when parents were invited to come to school and sort of hang out, or play with the kids. My mom did a wonderful thing that day. She gathered lots of kids around her and started telling a story. The story was about UFOs and friendly aliens coming to our planet to help guide us toward spiritual evolvement. More and more kids kept coming up, listening to her story. Back in those days most people did not believe in UFOs, or felt that they were cruel, evil, alien beings. My little friends and I were all surprised when Mama told the story about how friendly and good and sweet these aliens were, and how they helped us along our path in life.

When I got older Mom and I would share a little touch of humor between us when I would call her "Spacey Mom." We both laughed whenever I did that. In fact, I believe I called her that on one of Astara's video tapes that we made together.

Watching the movie ET again made me remember watching it with Mom and Dad. At the end of the movie, when ET is about to fly back to his home planet, he touches his finger to his heart, which glows and takes the glowing finger to the forehead of Elliot, his loving and dear, little friend who helped take care of and save ET while he was here on Earth, and helped him phone home. ET said to Elliot, "I'll be right here."

And when I saw that movie again I could feel dear, sweet Mama touching her finger to her heart and then to my head saying, "I'll be right here."

She will always be right here in my head and heart, dear reader, as well as here for every spiritual seeker, helping to guide us along the path. Even though she's "spacey," she's up there now with those good, Divine beings who will always be right here for us.

14

Nature

When I was a little girl, I grew up in Los Angeles. Growing up in the middle of a city has its pluses and minuses, as I'm sure you know, dear reader. But I got such joy out of hearing my parents stories of my father growing up in Indiana and Ohio, and my mother growing up in a small town in Texas.

My parents never told me to do this, but from their stories I got such inspiration from nature, that I would go into the back yard where there were several trees. I would talk to the trees either out loud or in my head and say things like, "Hello tree, thanks for being here, thanks for your beauty and your shade." And I would almost hear the tree talk back to me. When I told my parents that I had done this, they encouraged me quite a bit and said that we are connected to all of nature and there is a Divine force in all of nature which connects to us in a healing, soothing, wonderful manner.

I learned more about this when my parents and I would go on vacation. We would almost always go down to Palm Springs and stay in a very special, little hotel where we went every year. Away from the city lights it was glorious to see the stars. My father would even sleep out under the stars on the patio of the little hotel, and I would love playing in the desert lot right across the street from the hotel, crawling over rocks, looking at the mountains and just enjoy being out there.

But the place where I really got my first taste of being immersed in the wonderful, Divine power of being in nature was in Ohio, at the place where my father grew up. The whole family visited back there when I was about ten. It's called The Seven Caves of Ohio, and it's located several hours northeast of Cincinnati on Route 50. My grandfather bought The Seven Caves in 1928, and my father grew up there from age fifteen on. My grandfather single-handedly turned this land into a nature resort where people could come and enjoy wonderful bits of nature. I remember enjoying so much the caves themselves as well as sitting by Rocky Fork Creek under the trees on the grass, watching the beautiful water flow by. That area used to be a sacred gathering ground for Native American Indians, and being there, I could feel their presence as well as the Divine wonderful spirit of nature which touched my soul.

When I was there I got to see my first firefly, which is now one of my favorite creatures on this earth. They bring light and joy and somehow are able to share that joy with all who see them.

So no matter where you live, dear reader, in the city or in the country, somehow get outside, when it's safe, and share in the connection to the Divine that the wonderful nature on this planet offers. My parents encouraged it and I just loved it, and still do.

15

Sing a Song

I grew up in a rather musical household. I was taught to truly appreciate music. It's something that's been true throughout my life on this earthly plane.

When I was tiny, my mother would put me in bed and send me off to sleep singing lullabies. Her favorite was, "You Are My Sunshine." My mom had a lovely voice. Before she met Daddy she was an actress in Hollywood and took both acting and singing lessons.

When I was a young girl, Daddy built a three-manual Artisan organ with stops all the way around, which means that it could make all different sounds and tones, producing lovely melodies. He would play every evening in the alcove of our home in Los Angeles, and I would sit in the living room listening to those sweet melodies.

He often told our family the story of how, when he was a boy, he played the drums in his high school marching band. He was so good he was taken into the high school band even though he was in junior high at the time. The first time he marched he was still learning what to do. The band from the opposing football team that day came together with his band on the field during half time. At the end of half time they each marched off the field in opposite directions. Daddy was concentrating so much on his drumming that he marched off with the other team's band. His parents were watching from the stands rather aghast, but proud of him for being so musical.

When I was a young woman, my mother's only hobby was making reel-to-reel tapes of songs from different 78 LP albums. She'd have one song from one album and one song from another, making lovely tapes that were hours long. She'd often play them through the speakers in our house, and it was so lovely. As I continued to grow up I, of course, learned the lyrics to many of these songs and my father often said that if I had a nickel for every word I could remember from a song, I'd be a multimillionaire.

Mom and Dad and I, as if this life were a grand musical, would often break out in song. We'd be driving, and when we knew Dad should turn right, Mom and I would just start singing, "A turn to the right, a little White Light, will lead you to my blue heaven." One of the three of us often broke out in song just for the heck of it. And we all found it sweet and enjoyable and wonderful.

Even when I was in my thirties, after getting a Ph.D. from Purdue, and living in Boston for a few years, I often came to visit my parents. When I lived in Boston, we always spoke on the phone regularly. I would be in my little apartment and the phone would ring. I'd pick up the phone and not hear a "Hello," but instantly Mom's sweet voice would be singing,

"I just called to say I love you," which was a well known song at the time by Stevie Wonder. Even now that song often goes through my head, as do things like "You Are My Sunshine," or "My Blue Heaven," or any of hundreds of others that we all used to share together.

I know, dear reader, that my mom is still calling from heaven singing, "I just called to say I love you." And she doesn't only do this for me, dear reader, but for all spiritual seekers. So if the phone rings in your head one day, it's Mama saying she loves you, and is trying to help you along the spiritual path.

16
This World and Another

When I was growing up and my mother heard something negative on the television news or something disturbing from someone with whom she was in a conversation she would say, "This world and another." It was a statement that meant to show her shock, disbelief or disappointment in whatever news she had just heard. I'm sure it was a Southern expression because my grandmother, who lived in Texas, often said it too. But when Mother would say it in front of me as I was growing up, she'd re-frame it in my mind by setting me down and explaining all about heaven and the Divine planes of light that we all have waiting for us. She'd often use that as a stepping stone to explain about reincarnation and karma and other spiritual lessons of life.

So, dear reader, when you are shocked by something, you can say, "This world and another," but use the saying instead to help erase your fear of death just as my dear mother did for me. We do have another world to look forward to and it's a wonderful place filled with Divine light and loved ones who have passed on. My mother waits for me in this other world. So we do have not only this world, but spiritual seeker, also another world to look forward to. My sweet mom, as well as anyone you love who has passed on, is waiting there to welcome all of us from this world to another.

17

Mine Eyes Have Seen the Glory

When I was a little girl I came to notice something that seemed like a photograph in my head. I would often close my eyes at night and see this still image, or it would come to me during the day, just like a picture. This vision was of a man in a blue uniform holding a gun rather casually in his hand and also casually jumping down into a ditch which I have learned, of course, is called a foxhole. He does not appear to be under attack, but to be rather casually getting ready for some up-coming battle.

After several years I told my parents of this picture that kept appearing in my head and they used this image as a tool to teach me about reincarnation. They said it was probably me in a past life during the Civil War as a Union soldier getting ready for battle. I have learned all through the years that they must be right, because I can quote easily from the Gettysburg Address, and whenever the *Battle Hymn of the Republic* is played for some reason, even when my right arm has been injured from radiation treatment, which I had to get to heal my brain tumor, I feel absolutely that I must stand and salute with my right hand. This even happened as recently as this past 4th of July when I was watching the Boston Pops Orchestra play on TV. They played the Battle Hymn of the Republic. I was sitting on my couch, and even with my injured right arm, I broke into tears, stood and saluted while the song was played.

I still have this picture in my head of this soldier and I'm so grateful that my parents have used it as a way to teach me one of the spiritual lessons of life. So I salute them as well, and the wonderful ways they've used tools to teach me all about the new age religion which is in my heart to this very day.

18

Unhappy Camper

I had a wonderful dinner last night with my dear friend, Susan. I met her and her husband, Bo, who's also a very dear friend, when we were all in graduate school at Purdue University, in Indiana. I was blessed when they asked me to be the godmother of their youngest child, Alexandra. She and her older brother and sister are angels, and as far as I'm concerned, the best kids on earth.

Susan was telling me the story of how Alexandra just returned from summer camp. And it struck me how different summer camp is today than when I was a little girl.

Alexandra, who is now eleven and a half, spent her time at camp learning how to water ski, how to snorkel, and how to mountain climb. The only time I tried to water ski, I was in graduate school, and all I learned was how to ski with my face in the water. I never could stand up. But Alexandra, being the wonderful athletic, artistic and intelligent child that she is, mastered and enjoyed everything that she did at summer camp.

Another memory came back from when I went to summer camp. A bunch of kids and I were sitting around the camp fire and the boys insisted on telling terrifying ghost stories. They ended the evening by saying, "Be careful, a ghost may come after you tonight." We girls retreated to our cabin and I was awake the entire night waiting for some *thud, thud, thud* just outside the door, and for some evil ghost to come into the cabin. I was so scared, I called my parents and asked if they'd come take me home. Thank goodness they agreed to, and they came and got me the next day. But once again, they were able to use what was for me, a scary event to teach me about life after death.

My parents taught me that there were not any evil ghosts, but instead they were all Caspers, the Friendly Ghosts. They explained how most spirits go into the light, and are drawn up to heaven and, of course, try to reach back to their loved ones to send healing, or to let them know that they're all right, and to send love to the loved ones left here on earth. Occasionally, if someone has died a violent death, through suicide or murder, the transition does take longer, and that's why there are such things as haunted houses.

Spirits are not evil, they are simply doing things such as making noise, lighting candles, or doing other things that help them resolve the issues around their death until they finally ask for help in going up to the light. Though some humans interpret these things as scary, these souls are not out to harm us at all. They're simply trying to resolve their own issues and to learn to ask Divine guidance to help them get up to heaven where they belong.

My own dear mother said, "Whenever I go, I hope to get back in touch with you, and I hope you're never scared of me."

Since her passing, she has found many ways to be in touch, and I appreciate every time I'm able to identify her spirit.

So again, in a metaphysical way, my parents were "ghost busters" because they did use a scary time to teach me a good spiritual lesson. And while I still was a rather unhappy camper, at least I beat everyone in a coed rowing contest. That, and my parents wisdom, leaves me with plenty to be proud of.

19

Common Folk

From the time I was a young girl until now, I have often read sweet letters or email, or somehow heard from people that have been so grateful to my parents for the wonderful work they have done. Their books, their lessons, Dad's sermons, Fire Initiation Ceremonies, the healing, have helped thousands around the world.

And yet, with all this adulation, my parents have never been egotistical about what they've done. They have never felt somehow grand about themselves, they have never behaved as the old story goes of one egotistical person speaking to another person saying, "Well, enough about me. Let's talk about you. What do you think of me?" They have always felt that they were blessed to be able to do the work that they have done, to channel so much information from the higher planes of life and to use it in many different ways to help people. Even in the doing of this they never expressed feelings that they were better than other people, but just "common folk," as my mother from Texas would say.

So I learned from them to try to do the best at whatever you can do, to do a good job and to help other people along the way, but not to feel like some kind of diva while you're doing it. And I bless their hearts for being such wonderful role models.

20

Here We Go

From when I was very young until this very day, except for the one year I missed, being so sick, I have always helped with the Christmas service at Astara. Back behind the curtains before we came out to do whatever presentation it was, the three of us would all do a group hug, and all of us in unison would say, "Here we go, to do the greatest thing in the world." That didn't mean that we were the greatest thing in the world, it meant we were going out to try to do our part in the service as well as we possibly could for the people who attended.

Some years we would read from the beautiful story named *The Other Wise Man.* Each of us would take different parts to read while we showed beautiful slides. Or sometimes, Mom would give part of the sermon, and so would Dad. But always, starting from when I was little, I read from Luke, chapter two, verse eight, and I read it so many times, I memorized it. The scripture begins, "And in the same country there were shepherds abiding in the field, keeping watch over their flock by night ..." When I was very small and reading this scripture to the congregation, you are supposed to quote from verse ten, "The angels came to them and they were sore afraid." But I goofed up and said, "And they were *sure* afraid." The whole congregation laughed. Ever since then, every time I've read the scripture I've loved doing it. And by gathering together before the service, to say what we were about to do, once again my parents were teaching me an excellent spiritual lesson.

It will really help you do anything well to say to yourself, "Here I go, to do the greatest thing in the world." And whatever you're doing, dear reader, even if you're sure afraid, it'll come out better than it would have if you hadn't cheered yourself on with this little spiritual prayer which comes from the minds of two mystics.

I was just blessed, and I still am blessed to be with them.

21
Sacred Sites

When I was thirteen my parents and I took a fabulous trip across the country. We often stopped at wonderful, sacred sites such as Montezuma's Castle in Arizona, and Serpent Mound in Southern Ohio. At each of these sites, my parents taught me how to recognize and soak in the Divine spiritual essence of the place. We often prayed and meditated at each site.

Then, when I was in my 30s, I was able to go on Astara's tour groups to many countries. I'm grateful to my big sister, Astara, for this because we never could have afforded to go to these places on our own. My parents were always simply employees of the mystical foundation they founded, so we never would have had enough money to go on our own because my parents drew modest salaries from Astara.

Joining what I consider to be wonderful tours filled with Astarians and their friends, I've been able to visit fabulous sacred sites with either my mother or father in Egypt, Greece, England, Ireland, Thailand, Israel. I've also been to South

Africa, Ghana, Medjugorje (Yugoslavia), Canada and Switzerland. At each sacred site, in each country, my father or mother would conduct a spiritual ritual which I assisted in doing for the entire group. Then they gave each person time to pray and meditate on their own. Because of my parents' teaching, I had learned how to soak up the sacred, Divine energy at each site, and it has been wonderful ever since.

Once again, I'm grateful to my parents for teaching me such important spiritual lessons that have enriched my heart and soul in so many ways ever since I was born. And I'm grateful to my big sister, Astara, as well.

22

What's in a Name?

When I was about four my parents decided to bring a little dog into our family. He was a standard size black poodle, and my parents named him Pepper. He was my younger brother until I was about seventeen, when he left us to go to the higher life. But when I was about ten, I asked my parents just out of curiosity why they named him Pepper and they said, "We asked him what his name was and he told us."

My mother also had the habit of naming her cars. The last car she ever had was named the Annabelle Lee, and again I asked my mom, "Where did you get that name?" She answered, "I asked her what her name was."

The first car I ever got was when I was about twenty. I was rinsing it off one day and I mentally asked it, "What's your name?" It's not like I heard a human voice, or that it opened its hood to answer me, but I heard in my head, the word Ariel, who was a character in Shakespeare's play, *The Tempest.*

Of course I'm not at all suggesting, dear reader, that cars have souls, but I believe we're hearing from our own subconscious what we'd like to name the car. I do believe that every living thing, even a tree or a blade of grass, has a life force in it, and that animals *do* have souls, and that we are connected to them. I believe this because of these spiritual lessons my parents taught me by asking Pepper what his name was.

If you have a name in mind the next time you get a puppy, kitty, or older animal from the pound, name it that. But if you don't know, ask it, and I'll bet it will tell you.

23

Shooting Stars

When I was about twelve my parents and I were vacationing, as we always did, in Palm Springs. I believe it was in August, and my parents read in the paper how on one particular hot August night there would be a bunch of shooting stars in the sky. That evening, we jumped in the car and drove out to the desert to get as far as we could from all city lights. Daddy pulled the car up on the shoulder of the road, and the three of us got out and were looking up at the sky.

We saw beautiful, lovely shooting stars that night, but we also saw people who drove by about every fifteen minutes. They stopped and pulled over by our car. They got out and said, "Are you hurt? Is your car broken down? Is everything all right?" We assured them that we were fine, and that we were just out there to see the shooting stars. They looked at us like we were crazy, which is something that I had gotten used to, given that at that time practically none of any Astarian beliefs were popular.

So once again, my parents used all of this as a teaching tool for me to feel deeply connected to the Divine spiritual lights above us, and around us. And also to feel grateful for the headlights and the kindness of strangers that simply stopped and asked if we needed help.

That night the meaning of the phrase "As above, so below" became clear to me with both the shooting stars above and the headlights of kind strangers below.

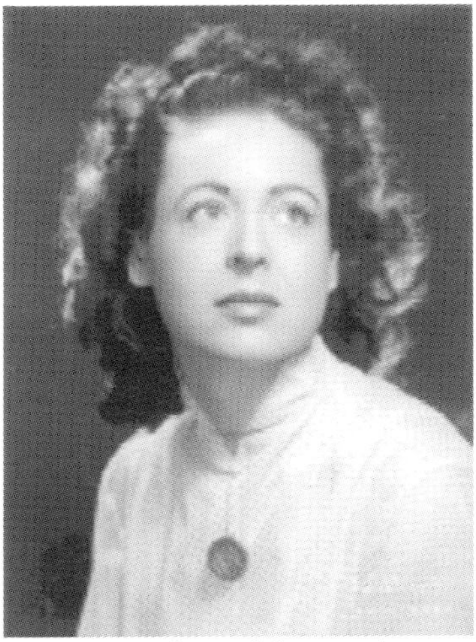 

Mom and Dad from photos dating back to the late 1940s.

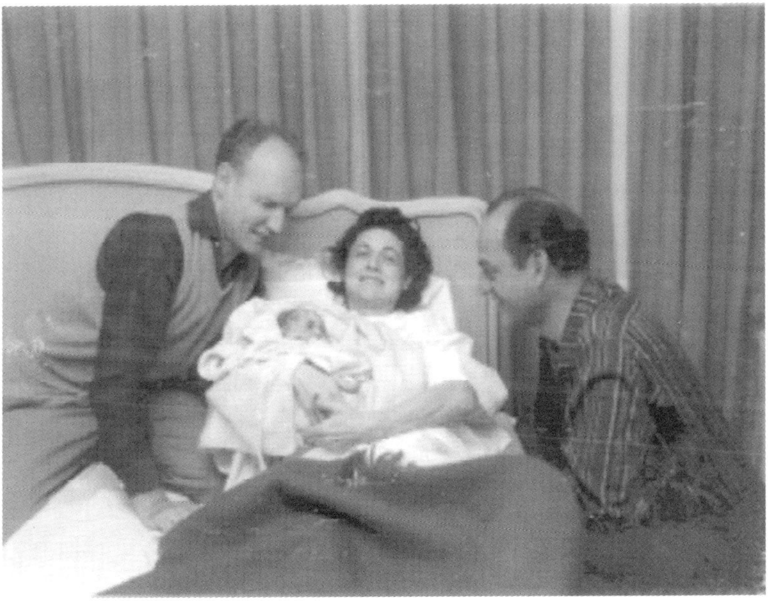

My arrival.

Me pulling Daddy's hair out.

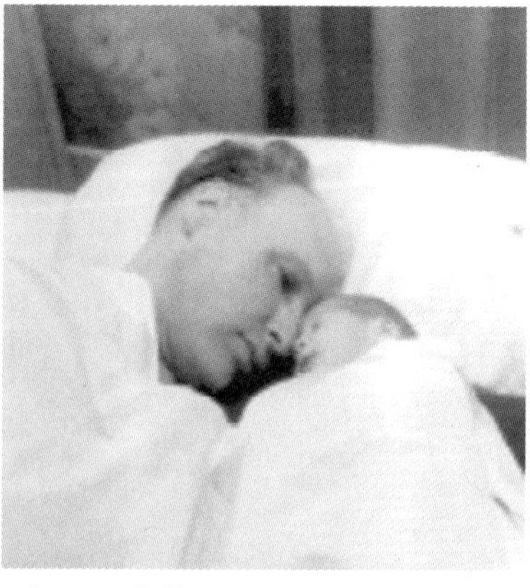

Early bonding with my folks.

My early fascination with spiritual Masters.

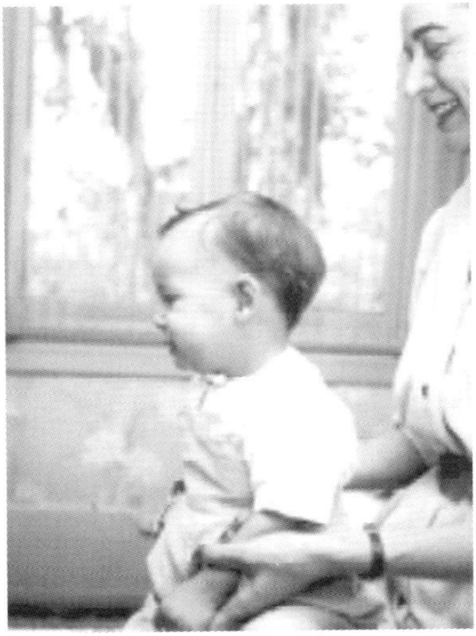

Mom and me watching TV.

On the platform at Astara's church.

Dad and I waiting to give a sermon.

There was always
music in our home.

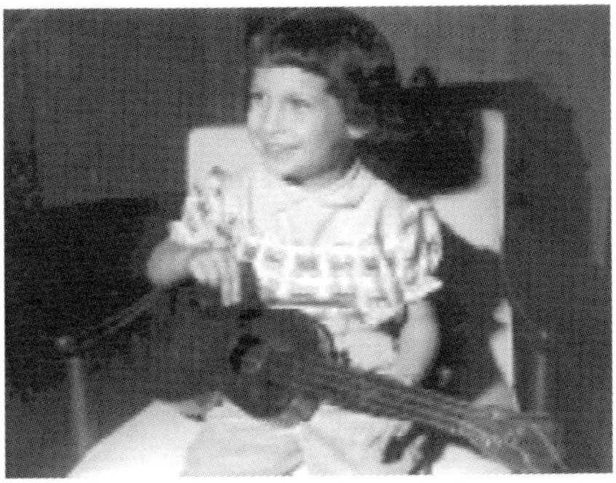

Holiday fun.

Typing my first novel.

Sita at the wheel.

Christmas at the Chaneys.

Learning the power of prayer.

Talking to Mother Nature.

Acting on my early fascination with the Civil War.

My nanny,
Margit Nilsson.

Mom introducing
me at church.

"Ammah"
(my father's mother),
Mom and me.

Daddy always took
pictures.

Behind Astara's
pulpit.

Mom and me
in the back yard.

At my college graduation ceremony.

Summer fun in Los Angeles.

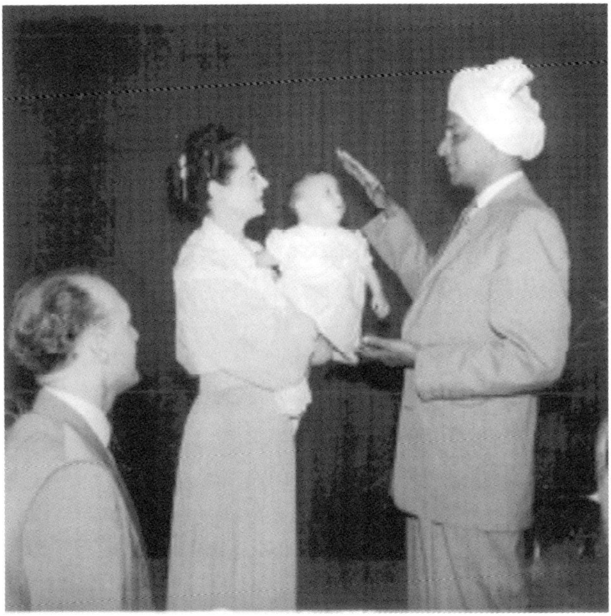

I met spiritual leaders throughout my life.

I had many opportunities to travel.
Above, South Africa. Below, Scotland.

Travelling with my Dad and Astara;
above, the Delta Queen on the Mississippi;
below, with Astarians in Thailand.

In later years,
relaxing, teaching
and spending time with Mom.

24

Sometimes You Have to Work at It

A teaching from one of my parents that started out to be a rather non-spiritual lesson has, to my mind, become one. My father has always been trying to teach me that "If you want to have fun, sometimes you have to work at it," meaning that if you're on vacation but not enjoying yourself particularly, or if you're going through the gentle ups and downs in life, fun won't just necessarily come to you. You have to get up and say, "Well, let's go to the mall today," or, "Let's go to the movies," or, "Let's go out to dinner. Let's do something fun." You have to be in charge of your own enjoyment.

An example of this occurred when I was about twelve and my parents and I were visiting many different places across the country, including Niagra Falls. We were having a wonderful time because it was so beautiful there. But Daddy decided to try to have even more fun in his own, sometimes peculiar way. We were visiting the wax museum there. My father says I was always enthralled by wax museums, and I wanted to go to all of them that we ran into. In the lobby of this wax museum, before you headed through the hallway into the exhibit hall, there was one chair on each side of the hallway door. While Mom and I were buying the tickets to go through the museum, Daddy went over and sat down on one of these chairs. He sat very still and quiet. Another family came in behind us and the little girl looked at Daddy and said to her parents, "Look how lifelike he is. Wow! Look, Mommy! These wax figures look like real." The little girl and her two parents moved up closer to Daddy as he sat very still and the little girl was about to reach out and touch him when he stood up, and they all screamed in surprise. After their shock they started laughing as Mom and I did too, and the girl's father shook my father's hand.

This was Daddy's way of working at having fun. I'm hopeful that this family still sees that as one of the highlights of their trip and not one of its scariest moments. But, we've always talked about that event and how "lifelike" Daddy looked.

Another way Dad chose to help us have fun on the trip was by going to the shop that would print a paper for you with any headline you chose. You could send this paper just like a postcard back to someone you love, or keep it yourself, to show how much you enjoyed your visit to Niagra Falls. Daddy chose a very special headline which left the entire staff and Mom and I laughing hysterically. He said to the man, "Make the headline read, quote, Aunty Biotic Goes Over the Falls in a Barrel." We took this newspaper back to my grandmother, who is my father's mother, to show her what a good time we had.

I've been able to take this lesson which says, "If you want to have fun, sometimes you have to work at it" and spiritualize it in my mind by telling myself that if I want to stay on this spiritual path, sometimes I have to work at it. I have to meditate, get out and bond with sweet Mother Nature, say prayers for myself, others and all of life on this planet and in this universe, continue reading spiritual books, attend spiritual seminars and really try my best to continue moving forward down the path. I'm not saying, dear reader, that one has to do all these things every day, but it's best to do a little bit of one or two of these things whenever possible.

So don't forget, if you want to have fun, sometimes you have to work at it, and if you want to keep moving down the spiritual path, sometimes you have to work at it. And don't forget to say a prayer for Aunty Biotic, who's gone over the falls and is well on her way downriver. Perhaps she'll end up in Hawaii having a wonderful vacation. And I hope that she's vacationing with the sweet family Daddy surprised at the wax museum.

25

Know Where You Are

A recent rash of child kidnappings on the news has made me remember an incident that happened to me when I was very young. When I was about six, Astara had hired someone who was both a handyman and a driver. Since my mother couldn't drive at that time, he would often drive her to different appointments, and he would also drive me to school and pick me up. Between his constant driving, he would be the handyman for Astara.

One day I had asked my parents if I could go to Griffith Park after school. They gave permission, as long as the man would stay with me and watch out for me. I remember we arrived at the park and we had to park the car several blocks away. I just happened to notice a church across the street from where we parked. He and I walked to the park and I played and walked along the little path in the park and, all of a sudden, I looked around and the man was gone. To this day I don't know what happened. Perhaps he stopped for coffee, or to talk to someone and I kept walking. In any event, I was totally lost, and there was no one there I knew.

My parents had taught me that if I was ever lost to head for the closest thing I knew. And our dear family friend, and my nanny, Margit, had always told me to remember where our car was parked, and go straight to it if I was ever lost. Suddenly I remembered the church across the street from the car and I could see from the park the steeple of the church. I headed right for it. And there, in the shadow of the steeple, was the car. Thankfully, the man had left it unlocked so I just got in and sat down, thinking now that he was lost. I waited and waited and waited.

Little did I know what was going on back in the park. The man had looked around and couldn't find me, and called my parents in a state of panic. And they called the police. My parents drove down to the park and joined the police in their car to slowly search through the park for little me. I just kept sitting in the car wondering when this man would come along. About an hour later either my mother or my father asked the police and this man if anyone had checked the car. They sort of dismissed the suggestion because they felt a child of my age never would have been able to remember where the car was parked, or how to find it. But my parents insisted. Finally, I looked out my window and there were my parents. They were deeply relieved, as was I.

The next time you feel lost in your life, dear reader, remember to ask your guardian angels to guide you toward the light of a holy place and wait there. You'll be safe, and the people who love you will find you. And you'll be there in the Divine Light.

Just as I'm glad I spotted that church steeple and had learned from my parents to head for something familiar, I was able to find my way and you can too, dear reader.

26

Stranglers in the Night

Ever since I can remember, at every church service at Astara, my parents made sure that the lyrics of the hymns we sung were changed to reflect Astara's beliefs. For example, a traditional lyric like, "Amazing Grace, how sweet the sound that saved a wretch like me." At Astara's service we always sang, "Amazing Grace, how sweet the sound that saved a *soul* like me." My parents always taught me that, of course, none of us are wretches. Every living being is a cell in the body of the Divine Being. We are all children of God, and while we're here on this school called Earth, though we do make mistakes, we're learning lessons and either slowly or quickly evolving spiritually to tap into the Divine Source that lives in all of us.

I have, of course, taken this lesson to heart. But what I also took to heart was a sometimes rather unspiritual way to change the lyrics to songs. This wasn't my parent's fault, except that as I have said before, we are a rather funny, musical family. In fun, I often change the lyrics to songs in my head. For example, the words of the song *Strangers in the Night* are "Strangers in the night, exchanging glances, wondering in the night, what were the chances we'd be sharing love before the night was through." In my head, I'd whimsically change the lyrics to, "Stranglers in the night, exchanging glances, wondering in the night what were the chances they'd be strangling each other before the night was through."

So, dear reader, remember you're not a wretch. You have the Divine Spirit within and around you, and I believe this with every fiber of my being because this is what my parents taught me. And I'm suggesting to you that you never exchange glances with stranglers in the night. Avert your eyes, dear reader, just avert your eyes!

27
Kippersita

When I was about fifteen, my Dad decided he should teach me about the evils of gambling. He talked it over with my Mom and they decided the best way to do this was for us all to go out to the Santa Anita Race Track and watch the horses race. They'd give me two dollars each race to bet on any horse I wanted to, and they figured that by losing all the money, I would learn the truth about gambling.

We went out to Santa Anita that day and I loved looking at the beauty of the horses as each one walked by. I chose the horse I would bet on to win by choosing the name of the horse that most appealed to me. Much to my parents chagrin, rather than loosing money, whatever horse I picked, about every other race, I won. And in fact, I almost won the trifecta, which would have been worth about $25,000. Still, we came home with several hundred dollars more than what we left the house with. I'm not suggesting, dear reader, that you should gamble. Even after this experience, I don't gamble. But because my parents had taught me about using intuition, that's what I used to choose the name that I liked best out of all the horses that were racing that day. And my intuition often proved correct. As I say, I don't use my intuition for such things as gambling, but for other spiritual things, as my parents taught me, as well.

One day, when I was in my late thirties and I was living on the East Coast, my father called me. He had been reading through his daily newspaper, and in the sports section he happened to notice a horse running at Santa Anita that day whose name was Kippersita. We happened to have a sweet little dog at the time named Kippy. Dad thought, "Oh, my gosh, with a name like Kippersita, I'll bet it will win." So I drove down to the race track nearest my home and bet two dollars on Kippersita. Unfortunately, Kippersita did not win, but it was a good idea and the horse had an interesting name that seemed to be connected to our family.

Dear reader, don't use your intuition or psychic ability to help you gamble, but use it to help you advance spiritually. And whatever you do, it's probably best not to bet on the trifecta.

28

My Medium Dad

As you may know, dear reader, my father used to work as a medium at Camp Chesterfield in Indiana. But a few years after he and Mom founded Astara, he stopped being a medium and moved on to run Astara, give wonderful sermons, and write terrific, spiritual books and lessons. But he still knows how to use his intuition quite well.

He proved this one day when he happened to be sitting on the hood of his car, which was parked at the curb outside my parent's home. The car, was parked on the street because we didn't have a driveway at that time. He was sitting on the car waiting for the mail carrier to arrive. But suddenly he thought, "I think I should go call Sita right now." I was living in Boston at the time. So he got up from sitting on the hood of the car and walked toward the house. When he got about half way to the house, a driver coming up the street lost control of his car and slammed it into my father's car. If he had still been sitting on the hood, Daddy would have been severely injured. But he still knew how to use his intuition to help protect him, and thank God he did.

You have your own intuition, dear reader, so when thoughts come to you suddenly, make sure they're not totally irrational, but if they are rational, listen to them, because they may be thoughts that come from above to help you. Both my parents taught me this in many ways, but the day Daddy got up from sitting on the hood of his car and decided to go in and call me right away, was a truly psychic, spiritual, saving moment. Which again taught me how close we all are connected to the Divine Spirit.

29

Born Laughing

As I mentioned before, dear reader, I was born at home. My parents insisted I be born at home because they couldn't stand hospitals and they wanted to welcome me into the nice, cozy world where I'd be living. It took them forever to find a doctor to come to the house, but, as I said before, they did finally find one although he slept through most of the labor and delivery.

He came in for the last five minutes of labor. My father, and my mother's sister, my Aunt Locky, had been helping for all the hours before I was emerging from the womb. When I finally emerged, 24 hours after labor began, the doctor was about to hit my little behind to get me to breathe, like they do with most babies. But he didn't have to do that because as soon as I came out of my sweet mother's womb, I looked at my sweet father and started laughing. I've been laughing at their wonderful sense of humor ever since.

What I've never laughed at is the wonderful way they have taught me spiritual lessons and to stay on the spiritual path and to believe in the Divine Spirit connecting us all. I'm so thankful to them for this, as well as for their wonderful personalities and fabulous senses of humor that have always been such a joy to live with.

30

Mom at the Way Station

I saw my mom last night. And it was really wonderful. I had a dream where I was flying in the front of a plane being piloted by our family friend and dentist -- the one who made such a beautiful video tape for Mom's memorial service. This video had beautiful, spiritual music and showed lovely scenes from nature symbolizing the cycle of life and transition very gently and naturally.

Anyway, the plane kept going up and up and up, until finally we arrived at a way station of some sort. There were lots of passengers on the plane and we all went into a large lounge waiting area. Very soon people started coming through the doors at the other side of the building. They'd just arrived at this way station, coming from the opposite direction.

Then, suddenly, I saw my mom come through the open doors. There she was, looking younger and healthy and happy, dressed in a beautiful gold dress. I was so surprised and thrilled to see her. We visited for quite awhile, and as seems to be usual for me, I can't for the life of me recall what we talked about, but I discovered my dad and two of my aunts had come with me on the plane. They each in turn got to visit with and spend time with Mom, too. Then I woke up.

I know this wasn't just a dream. I often pray for my mom and ask to visit her and be able to remember it the next morning, if it's for the highest good. And I know this was just such a visit. To be honest, I don't remember dreaming of her or visiting her that often -- I wish I did. But maybe it would be harder in some way if I remembered more.

It is May as I write this, and since May is the anniversary of her transition, and when we celebrate Memorial Day, I wanted to share my visit with you. I know she's with me, loving me, healing me, supporting me far more often than I remember. And I know she's with you, too, whenever you call on her, as are all the people you love who've gone ahead of us both past that way station. They're with us and we're with them, praying for, supporting, laughing with and loving each other. And that's just right. That's just as it should be.

31

Stay on 95

When I was about eight years old, my Mom and Dad and I took a trip across the country. We would stop at various places for them to put on seminars, which many Astarians attended. We made our way from California to New York by train, plane and car. Once we arrived in New York, we headed down through Boston to Washington D.C., sightseeing along the way in between their seminars.

Neither of my parents were the best of navigators, nor was I at that age, nor am I today. We'd often have to stop and ask directions to get to our next hotel or to the next seminar or tourist site we wished to see. Inevitably, the person of whom we would ask directions would at first say, "Stay on 95," and then tell us directions to our destination.

This became a never-ending joke in our family through the years, particularly to me. When I would lose the keys to the car, or other personal item, when I would have trouble with school work, or professional work as I grew older, when I would have difficulty with relationships, the first sort of light piece of advice from my parents would be to "Stay on 95." As I am older now, I look at the esoteric meaning behind this cute phrase.

At times when you feel lost, troubled, experiencing a difficult time, turn to meditation, prayer, ongoing spiritual study through books, lessons, cassette tapes. Sit down with friends or family, or a therapist, to talk things through. You will be continuing on your spiritual journey and what will you be doing? What my parents always told me to do, you'll be "staying on 95," and you'll make it.

32
Rituals

Often, when I think of ritual, I think of something with spiritual significance. The lighting of a candle every morning before a morning prayer, the ritual of a meditation practice, or repeating certain sacred words at specific times. I believe a great deal in ritual, and know that there is tremendous spiritual, emotional, mental and physical light and power contained within them waiting for our participation.

But as I began to think about ritual, I realized that some of the most important ones of my life haven't really had a spiritual context. One of my favorite memories of graduate school is regularly meeting all my friends at the "Ground Round" on Thursday nights to laugh, enjoy one another and share stories of the week's classes and activities. Then we'd eventually make our way across town to the "Stabilizer" to hear Cool Ray and the Polaroids play great blues and old time rock and roll. Thursday nights for five years were great. All of my Thursday night crowd have become lifelong friends and somehow even now, when most of us live far apart, the arrival of Thursday night still feels kind of sweet.

I developed a sweet ritual with my parents, too, when I used to fly into town for visits, which was very often. Mom and I loved to watch movies together, so almost every night of my visit I'd go to the video store, pick out something I was pretty sure she'd like, bring it home and we'd spend a great evening together eating popcorn and watching movies. Dad, who's not such a movie buff, but wanted to be with us, usually struggled to stay awake through part of the show and then fell asleep on the couch. What a wonderful time the three of us had.

I now have a ritual with my dad. Every Sunday night we've taken to getting take-out food, bringing it back to my apartment and eating dinner on my patio as the evening slips by. It feels almost like a picnic and it's something we both look forward to through the week.

All these are simple things. Some of these kind of rituals just happen and others you need to plan and do a little something to create. I really encourage you to develop these kinds of rituals with the people you love. Do something every week, even the same time of the week, that you really look forward to. Know that you have that time of laughter, fun and sweetness coming up.

Commit yourself to creating these kinds of rituals that are not only spiritual, but that are social, relational and emotional in nature, as well. Believe me, they'll enhance your spiritual life. And they'll give you some of the best times you'll ever have.

33

Mom Now

I think about my mom all the time. I talk to her. I listen to her. I miss her and yet feel her with me, sometimes very strongly, sometimes just a step or two away as she's busy helping and supporting others. But always nearby, just as she was when she was here.

As you may have experienced yourself, it's hard to even conceive of life going on when someone who you love so much is no longer right here with you. It somehow doesn't seem possible to go on living without that person on this earth.

But we do go on. And the relationship goes on and develops, too. And we adjust to the new and different ways of connection. And to the times when we feel too much apart and just have to know that we aren't, really.

I try to think about ways to keep the relationship between us growing. I have several pictures of my mom and me around the house. Sometimes I'll bring her flowers, just like I used to do, and put them beside one of the pictures. I'll light a candle for her. I'll talk out loud to her, updating her on things going on in my life as I walk around the house or drive in my car. I'll often just stop and listen and sometimes hear her voice or get an inner impression about what she's telling me. I will occasionally pray as I go to sleep that I can go visit her that night and that I remember it in the morning. And sometimes that's exactly what happens.

I tell you all this because I think it's important that we here on earth do our part to maintain the relationship, to stay open to and to strengthen the connection, just as we need to do with all our important relationships on this plane. We shouldn't just wait to hear from the Otherside, expecting some departed one whom we love to do all the work and then wonder why they never call or write. So do all you can to nurture the relationship.

I will tell you, the connection will never feel strong enough, or constant enough or "real" enough as things are "real" on this plane, simply because we want it to be as it always was, and that just can't be. But what can be is a still growing, vital relationship where love, support, healing, and even laughter is given and received. And this ongoing connection is such a comfort and such a joy. It also gives us assurance that our lives will go on long past that moment called death — and what a gift that is.

So, thanks, Mom, for all that you do to stay close to me and look after me, like you always said you would. You're doing a great job.

34

My Dad's Sermons

Whenever I attend Sunday church service with my father giving the sermon I love it when he starts out by saying, "When I was a boy...". My favorite sermons are about his own childhood stories, although I love all his sermons. I would like to tell you a few stories he never used in sermons.

On the day that he was born, October 27, 1913, his grandparents planted a cherry tree in their back yard. They believed that as the tree grows, so will the person. Fortunately, my sweet father grew to be even stronger, more handsome, and healthier than the tree. But it was a lovely tree and he often played under its beautiful shadow when he was growing up. So, dear reader when something important happens in your life, punctuate it by either planting a tree which connects you with our dear, sweet Mother Nature or make a note in your journal, go out and celebrate the occasion, pray about it, meditate on it, or buy something that would be symbolic to have in your home to mark the wonderful event. This cherry tree was always important in his grandparent's, his parent's and his life. So do something that will really mark an important day in your life. My bet is that when my sweet father makes his transition to heaven, a beautiful cherry tree will be waiting for him there, along with loved ones.

Some of the stories Dad tells reflect the great sense of humor that ran in his family. I'm fortunate that my mother and her family had a wonderful sense of humor, too, which has been passed down to me.

One way that my great-grandfather expressed his sense of humor was that he and my great-grandmother would invite people over to the house for dinner, or for a get together or for a party, and when someone would ask to use the rest room they would tell them that the rest room was upstairs. Guests who had never visited the house would walk up the stairway, turn left on a landing to walk up a second stairway, turn right to go up a third stairway, and just as they were turning right would see in the shadows a huge grizzly bear with his paw raised as if in attack. They would scream and then they would laugh, discovering, of course, that it was a stuffed bear. And my great-grandparents downstairs would laugh at the same time.

On our road up the spiritual pathway, dear reader, we all symbolically encounter grizzly bears. But, as they say in the Bible, "Fear not." For the grizzly bear will not attack you, he's simply there to give you pause with his paw, which at first will frighten you and, as time goes by, you shall feel better about it, or laugh at what happened. The spiritual path can be marked with these frightening moments, but we all get past them, moving onward using prayer, meditation or good relationships, or just focussing on our own goals along the pathway. Don't worry, dear reader, you'll make it to the rest room and beyond.

Another story I like is about Dad playing baseball as a teenager. He happened to trip over the second baseman's foot while he was running the bases and broke his arm. They had to put a cast on. But my father, being the adventurous person that he is, decided he did not want to let that deter him. He went out to the garage and got out an old bicycle which must have belonged to his grandparents. The bicycle's tires were completely deflated, but for some reason my dad decided to try and ride it anyway. He rode it around the front yard of his grandparents home and suddenly realized that with his broken arm he was afraid to stop the bike because he may fall off. So he rode around and around and each time he passed the front porch, he would yell out, "Help!" Finally his grandmother heard him and came out the door to stand in front of the bike and catch him so he would not fall over.

When you're on your spiritual path, dear reader, and are going through a fearful time, call for help from loved ones who have passed on, or from your Master Teachers, or from your guardian angels. Someone will be there to help you in any way possible. But, again, while on your spiritual path, do not ride with deflated tires, but inflate your tires with love , prayer, meditation, spiritual time with mother nature, reading metaphysical books, or whatever way you can. And it's best if you discover how to apply your own brakes so that you don't fall over. But, regardless, someone's always there to help all of us, no matter what.

35

Right Car, Right Relationships

I've told you about some of our vacations in Palm Springs. One time driving down there we were about to run out of gas, so my dad pulled the car into a gas station. My mother used the opportunity to get out and visit the women's room.

After my father had filled the car with gas he noticed another car behind him that was waiting to get to the pump. So Daddy pulled our car over to the side to wait for Mama. I was sitting in the back seat and saw her come out of the women's room and get in the other person's car. Fortunately, she got out in just a minute or two and headed over to our car, laughing. What had happened was that she mistook the stranger's car for ours, got in without looking, and said, "Let's go!" and then turned to her left to look at a strange man staring at her in shock. She had then apologized and gotten out to look for and find our car.

When you're on the spiritual path, dear reader, make sure you're in the right relationships with good, loving, respectful people that would never abuse you, but love you the way you deserve. Stay on your spiritual path in whatever way you choose so that you don't get in the wrong car and say "Let's go!" to be kidnapped and driven off by a stranger. Say "Let's go" and then laugh about it and get back on the right track again with the right people who love you, support you and respect you, as you do them. Keep on going, dear reader, you'll reach your destination.

36

Lights in the Forest

The house in Los Angeles in which I was born and where I grew up was lovely because my parents had a wallpaper hanger who was also an artist, and he painted beautiful pictures on the wallpaper downstairs in the living room as well as in my bedroom upstairs. In both places he painted beautiful wooded scenes as if we were living in and I was sleeping in gorgeous woods. Downstairs there was also beautiful Divine Light coming down into the woods from heaven.

In my bedroom there also hung a gorgeous painting which I still have of a young girl walking through the woods with gentle, loving animals around her such as a deer, a rabbit, a squirrel and a horse and she has floating above her guardian angel. My sweet parents used all this beautiful artistry to teach me that we all have guardian angels and even if we're walking through the darkness of the woods, there may be danger, but we also have safe, spiritual animals connected to our Mother Earth around us and sweet guardian angels to help guide our steps.

We also have the Divine Light streaming down from heaven no matter what. It's our job to stay on the spiritual path, to ask for help when we need it, to pray for our Mother Earth and all forms of life on it, and to pray for ourselves when we need it. Our guardian angel is there, and the Light is there, it's just waiting for us to do our part.

37

A Pat on the Head

When I was in my twenties and thirties and visiting my parents at our home, we often sat and watched TV in the evening with Mom sitting in a chair to my left and Dad lying on the couch to my right. Whenever Mom would get up to leave the room for something, she had to walk past my chair to get out into the kitchen and the rest of the house. She would always pat me on the head as she passed by.

I have noticed in the years since her passing that oftentimes if I'm watching something rather mystical on TV, listening to meditative music, or reading a spiritual book, I feel a tingling on the left side of my head. It doesn't feel like a hand on my head, but just a tingling on my left side where Mother used to sit. When I feel that I've learned to stop and say "Thank you, Mom" because I know it's a healing, loving touch, an encouraging touch from on high from my dear mother. Please know that my mother and our other Astarian Master Teachers are there not only for me, but, of course, for you as well.

So any time you are in some crisis in your life, or pursuing your spiritual path, whether you know it or not, Mom or another of our Master Teachers is patting you on the head, whether you feel it or not, and sending healing and encouragement and love.

"Keep going, seeker," is the message from above, and if you try hard, I'll bet you feel it. And we at Astara send our pats on the head to you, too.

38

Big, Bad Me and Mickey D

When I was a teenager I did what most teenagers do. I acted out. Because of the way my parents raised me to treat my body as a temple, I didn't smoke or drink, or take drugs, or have sex, or anything like that. Even after I turned twenty-one, I would only have one alcoholic beverage on ocassion. Because my parents had raised me to be a vegetarian, one of the ways I acted out was by going to McDonald's. I never told my parents, but occasionally I would have a hamburger and fries and a Coke. And that was my little way of being rebellious.

I'm no saint, but I was brought up to meditate, to pray, to be in touch with Mother Nature, and with the higher dimensions of life. I was also taught never to abuse my body, and never to allow anyone else to do so. I was taught to stand up for myself, and for the Divine spirit within me.

We all have the Divine spirit within each of us so stand up for yourself, dear reader, and your body, as well as for any dear friends around you. Never let anyone abuse or mistreat you in any way. Stay on the spiritual path, and if you do, perhaps the greatest temptation you'll face is the question: "Would you like cheese with that?"

39

Broken Window Reflections

Several years ago, during one of my frequent cross-country trips to visit my parents, we got a call at about 7:30 at night. Some kids had thrown rocks at a window in Astara's mail room. The window had broken, the alarm went off and Upland's finest were responding. Dad and I had to respond too, by going down to meet them.

I was annoyed because it was the last night of my visit and I needed to pack and do a thousand other things. The kids were, of course, nowhere to be found. After the police left, I called a 24-hour glass repair person. Dad and I sat down to wait on the steps of Evergreen Lodge. A promised half-hour wait stretched to one-and-a-half hours.

But it was a warm and clear night out. As we sat there and as the time went by Dad started talking about his relief and optimism about Astara's future since we sold some campus property, which is directly across the street from where we were talking.

Also, he spoke of his plan to go back to his alma mater, Miami University of Ohio. He had been the drum major when he was a young man in college, and now he was going to homecoming to be the drum major of the Alumni Band. There he will be I thought, twirling the baton, leading the band in the loud and wonderful Miami University fight song, hearing the music from all those instruments swelling behind him, marching across the green of the football field. And I thought, I hope when I'm 80 years old, I have plans to do something equally wild and wonderful.

Sitting there with my dad sent me again to a place of deeper appreciation for both my parents. The ways they have lived their lives have been truly remarkable. I see my mom, day after day, work tirelessly to write a new book, edit and update a Lesson, consider how to put together the new videotape, make decisions about the complicated business aspect of Astara, pray for someone's healing over a prayer petition. They are both so alive and committed to Astara and to you.

So, much as I sometimes worry about my dad out there marching around on the football field, I'm inspired by his sense of fun, by his taking time for himself. I'm inspired by the way both my parents have lived their lives with love, doing work they cherish for the service of others. So, what could have been one-and-a-half hours of annoyance and upset was transformed into a time of appreciation and love of my folks and a reminder about how to truly live life. May you and I also incorporate the Spirit of our spiritual beliefs into our own lives in ways that enrich us, bringing joy to ourselves and those around us.

40

I've Been Truly Blessed

When I was about eight years old, on a trip across the country we made a stop in Camp Chesterfield, Indiana.

Camp Chesterfield is a spiritualist camp outside Indianapolis in a little town appropriately named Chesterfield. Being a spiritualist camp means that it's a camp where many wonderful psychics and mediums do their work. We stopped there because my father had worked there as a medium for thirteen years. I was so proud to see how the other mediums who were his dear friends greeted him and greeted us all, and took me off to the side to tell me what a wonderful psychic and medium he had been.

In Camp Chesterfield there's a large quad which is, of course, a lovely area filled with grass and trees where they had small round stone tables where a medium would sit and do individual readings for people. The table where he used to sit had his lovely name carved on top of it. My father told me that he wasn't quite as good at individual readings as he was with group readings. And if you've ever seen *Crossing Over* with John Edward on TV, or James Van Praagh, you'll know what he means. That's what my father did back in the forties. And so many people came up to tell me he had done it so well. As Dad has told me, there are good mediums and bad mediums and even a good medium has his or her good days and not so good days, just like anyone has in any profession.

Camp Chesterfield is a beautiful place filled with sweet little houses where the mediums live on the grounds. There's the wonderful quad with many places to sit and pray or meditate, including a Trail of All Religions, and many other sacred places. All these things were a joy to me to see, but my biggest joy was seeing the porch of a little house on the grounds, for it was on this porch that my sweet parents first met in 1947. It was a joy for me to sit there and be so grateful that my parents had met, and in fact they married three months later. Some people said the marriage wouldn't last because they married so soon after they had met, but in fact, the marriage did last quite happily, and my mother passed on just a few months before what would have been their 50th wedding anniversary. After she passed I was looking for something in her room and I came upon a journal that was in a drawer of her bedside table. I certainly didn't read most of the journal because I thought that was her personal property and it was not for me to look back on her personal life when she was 20 and 30 to find out what happened. It was none of my business. But I did read the last page of her journal which was written on the day she met my father. The journal ends saying, "Today I met a wonderful medium named Robert Chaney. I looked into his eyes and my heart was filled with amazement and joy." Even though this comment about meeting my father was about in the middle of thc entire journal book, she never wrote a page after that and kept this journal by her bed all through the years.

So dear reader, in a similar way I want to say that my heart, my soul have been filled with amazement and joy by being so blessed as to grow up with these two people who have been amazing psychics, and writers, and teachers, and healers and fabulous parents. I've been truly blessed.

The publisher of this book is a nonprofit organization presenting metaphysical, mystical, philosophical and self-help material. For more information on Astara or additional books by any of Astara's authors, write:

Astara Administration Building
P.O. Box 5003
Upland, CA 91785

E-MAIL: **mail@astara.org**

WEBSITE: **www.astara.org**

Note from the Publisher ...

Copies of this book are also available on audio tape and CD at bookstores or direct from the Publisher.